Wash Your Hands!

Published in the United States of America by Cherry Lake Publishing
Ann Arbor, Michigan
www.cherrylakepublishing.com

Reading Adviser: Marla Conn MS, Ed., Literacy specialist, Read-Ability, Inc.
Book Design: Jennifer Wahi
Illustrator: Jeff Bane

Library of Congress Cataloging-in-Publication Data

Names: Marsico, Katie, 1980- author. | Bane, Jeff, 1957- illustrator.
Title: Wash your hands! / by Katie Marsico ; [illustrator] Jeff Bane.
Description: Ann Arbor, Michigan: Cherry Lake Publishing, [2019] | Series:
My healthy habits | Audience: K to grade 3. | Includes bibliographical
references and index. Identifiers: LCCN 2018034522| ISBN 9781534142756 (hardcover) |
ISBN 9781534140516 (pdf) | ISBN 9781534139312 (pbk.) | ISBN 9781534141711
(hosted ebook) Subjects: LCSH: Hand washing--Juvenile literature. | Hand--Care and
hygiene--Juvenile literature. Classification: LCC RA777 .M2693 2019 | DDC 613/.4--dc23
LC record available at https://lccn.loc.gov/2018034522

Printed in the United States of America
Corporate Graphics

About the author: Katie Marsico is the author of more than 200 reference books for children and young adults. She lives with her husband and six children near Chicago, Illinois.

About the illustrator: Jeff Bane and his two business partners own a studio along the American River in Folsom, California, home of the 1849 Gold Rush. When Jeff's not sketching or illustrating for clients, he's either swimming or kayaking in the river to relax.

How do we color pictures?

How do we eat pizza?

How do we greet people?

We use our hands!

Our hands also spread **germs**.

Most germs are too tiny to see.
Yet some make people sick.

There are many ways germs get on our hands.

Sometimes germs travel when people cough or sneeze.

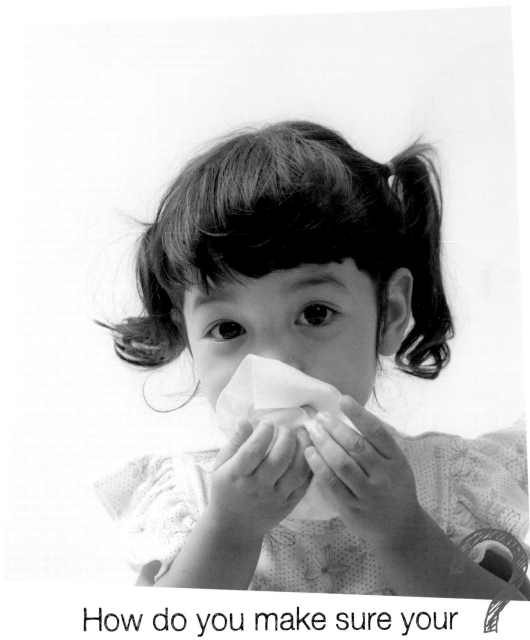

How do you make sure your hands stay clean?

Germs are found in bathrooms.

Handling **raw** food spreads them.

Touching garbage does, too.

Even petting animals spreads germs.

Hand washing stops the spread of germs. It is a good **hygiene** habit.

Always try to follow a few hand-washing rules.

First, wet your hands with clean, running water.

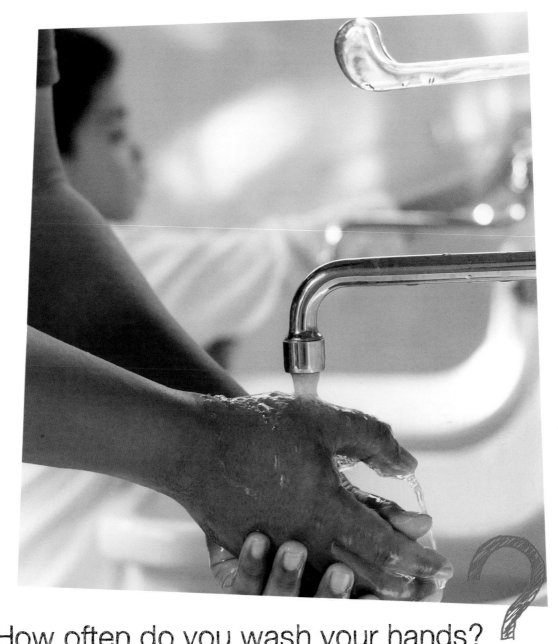

How often do you wash your hands?

Next, **lather** up.

Get soap between your fingers and under your nails!

Do this for at least 20 seconds.

(Time yourself by humming the "Happy Birthday" song twice.)

Afterward, rinse your hands in clean water.

Finally, be sure to dry them.

Some people use **hand sanitizer** instead.

Soap and water are often better, though. They kill more germs.

Hand washing keeps us healthy.

It also **prevents** us from passing germs to others!

What are some of your healthy habits?

glossary

germs (JURMZ) tiny organisms that often cause disease

hand sanitizer (HAND SAN-ih-tye-zuhr) a special liquid used to clean hands (instead of soap and water)

hygiene (HYE-jeen) keeping yourself clean or other actions that support good health

lather (LATH-ur) to use soap and water to work into a thick foam

prevents (prih-VENTS) stops something from happening

raw (RAW) uncooked or undercooked

index